CREATIVE WRITING JOURNAL VOLUME 1

Clever Prompts for Clever Children

Copyright © 2020 Carolyn Cohagan

All rights reserved.

No part of this publication may be reproduced, distributed, or transmitted in any form or by any means, including photocopying, recording, digital scanning, or other electronic or mechanical methods, without the prior written permission of the publisher, except in the case of brief quotations embodied in critical reviews and certain other noncommercial uses permitted by copyright law.

For permission requests,

please address Girls With Pens.

Girls With Pens

PO Box 301894

Austin, TX 78703

ISBN: 978-0-9995624-7-5

Welcome to your new writing journal!

When I was a girl, I was always receiving blank diaries and journals as gifts. I loved the way they looked with their fancy covers and clean white pages, but there was one problem. I never knew what to write! Those blank pages were intimidating and my blank journals sat around gathering dust, which is why I decided to create a journal that is specially made for creative writing. Inside, I have shared my students' favorite prompts from my writing camps and workshops. My mother, painter Lynn Cohagan, and I had a wonderful time creating the accompanying images to jump start your imagination.

I hope you have as much fun filling in this journal as we had making it. And please feel free to send me your favorite story at carolyn@kidswithpens.org. I'd love to share it on the Kids With Pens blog!

Sincerely,

Sir Bruce has been stuck in this jar for 200 years. Write the story of how and why he got trapped there.

You go to school tomorrow and something is dramatically different. No one notices but you. Write about the day.

There is a spider who works at the Empire State Building in New York City. Today he is going to get fired. Tell the story of what happens.

I love to create villains. I bet you'll like it, too. Write a story from a villain's point of view. The only rule is somewhere in the story you must use the phrase "Beware, children."

A pink hippo and purple gorilla live in the jungle. Neither of them has any friends because they are strange colors. They don't like each other because hippos and gorillas don't get along. What happens when these two realize they are going to have share the same watering hole?

A little known fact is that before Neil Armstrong landed on the moon, Sidney the Chicken was sent to check out the scene. Write about his experience when he landed and his difficulties getting home.

* Thank you to Lila Wilson for her beautiful drawing of a chicken. For a drawing of your own adorable pet, please visit www.wildthingsinart.com

Tell a story from the perspective of someone or something very small who is arriving at a location for the first time (a library, a carnival, a museum, a rodeo, etc.)

The ancient Greeks often combined animals in their myths to create fascinating characters like Medusa, the Chimera, or the Minotaur. Combine three unlikely animals to create a brand new creature. Tell the story of this creature's difficulties trying to make friends with other animals.

This pug was always told she was too little to go on a big adventure, but today she decided to prove the other dogs wrong. Who joins her and what problems do they face?

In a garden in the middle of London is a secret door to a magical land. Tell me about discovering the door and your adventure when you arrive in the new world. I want as many details as possible about what things look like and what is different in the magical land.

There once was a fish who dreamed of flying in the sky. One day a child's kite flew close to the water and the fish jumped aboard it. The fish was so happy he decided never to return to the sea. What happens next?

While going through their uncle's attic, two siblings discover a strange map. Their uncle vanished many years ago, and they think this map may hold the secret to his disappearance. What do they do with the map?

If you would like to hear about future creative writing books, Carolyn's novels, or her writing camps, you can sign up for her newsletter at
www.girlswithpens.org

You can also follow us on Instagram!

Lynn Cohagan is @austinlynn308

Carolyn Cohagan is @carolyncohagan

www.ingramcontent.com/pod-product-compliance
Lightning Source LLC
Chambersburg PA
CBRC090838010526
44118CB00008B/249